Whose TRACK Is That?

by **Stan Tekiela**

Adventure Publications
Cambridge, Minnesota

Dedication

To Abby, with all my love.

Front Cover: (bear paw) by Susan Kehoe/shutterstock.com; (white-tailed deer) by Stan Tekiela; (bobcat) by Stan Tekiela; (raccoon) by Robynrg/shutterstock.com
Back Cover: (Canada goose foot) by sunakri/shutterstock.com; (rear foot of raccoon) by Foxy71/shutterstock.com; (puppy paw) by oksana2010/shutterstock.com; (bullfrog hind foot) by Stan Tekiela
Inside flap: (bullfrog front foot) by Stan Tekiela
All photos by Stan Tekiela except pg. 35 by Jonathan Poppele; pg. 39 by Pat Stornebrink/shutterstock.com; pg. 47 by Jonah Evans/ https://www.flickr.com/photos/22982999@N03/14375991930/; pg. 51 (handprint) by ucubestudio/shutterstock.com

Illustrations by Julie Martinez and Bruce Wilson except Bullfrog, Canada Goose, and Robin by Jonathan Poppele

Cover and book design by Jonathan Norberg

10 9 8 7 6 5 4

Whose Track Is That?
Copyright © 2020 by Stan Tekiela
Published by Adventure Publications
An imprint of AdventureKEEN
310 Garfield Street South
Cambridge, Minnesota 55008
(800) 678-7006
www.adventurepublications.net
All rights reserved
Printed in China
ISBN 978-1-59193-958-0 (pbk.)

WH🐾SE TRACK? Is That?

It's a PHOTOGRAPHER!

I love taking pictures of animals, but it's not always easy.
Sometimes I can't find the animals. When this happens,
I only get pictures of their tracks....

This animal's track is long and skinny and might loop or curl about.

Sometimes, it's a straight line.

Whose track is that?

HINT: You might see a Robin pull one from your lawn.

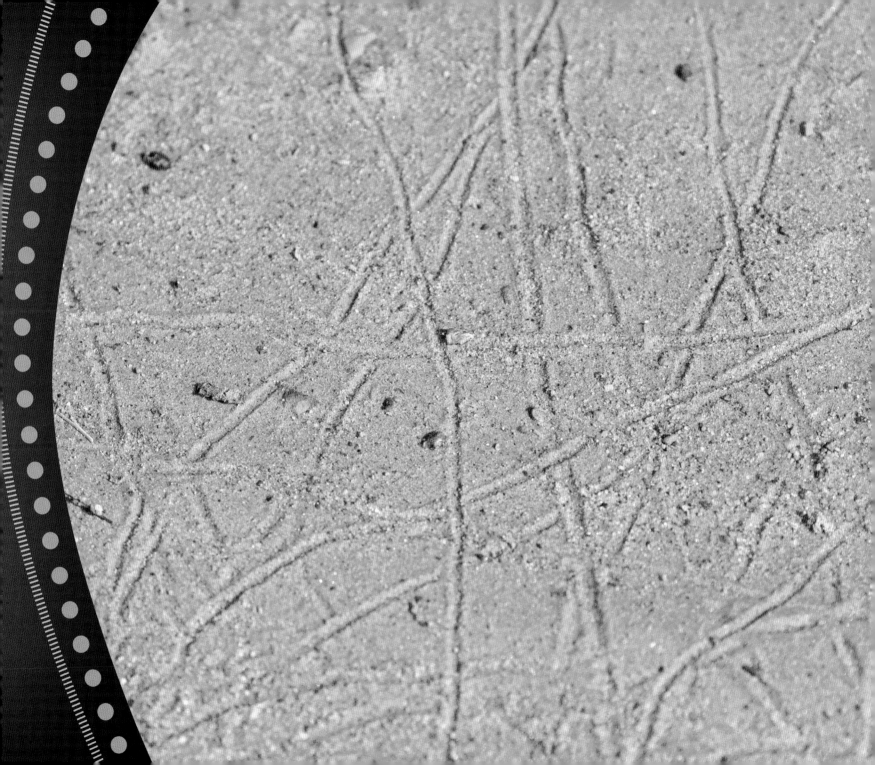

It's an EARTHWORM!

Earthworms usually live underground, but they often come out when it rains. Even though they don't have any bones or a hard outer covering like insects, worms are strong enough to burrow into the soil and leave tracks!

Pointed on one end and rounded on the other, this track is heart shaped.

This animal's hooves are extra hard and make deep tracks in the mud.

Whose track is that?

HINT: You might see this large animal running through fields or parks.

It's a
DEER!

The **White-tailed Deer** is the most common large animal in America. Male deer, known as bucks, grow a new set of antlers every year. In late winter, the antlers fall off; mice and voles love to chew on the old antlers, but sometimes you can find them in fields!

Small and round, my tracks are not easy to spot.

My claws don't stick out, so my tracks don't leave claw marks in the mud or snow.

Whose track is that?

⟶

HINT: This animal looks like a large house cat.

It's a
BOBCAT!

Bobcats are small cats, not much larger than a house cat. They are found in a wide variety of habitats, from forests to wetlands. When a bobcat walks, its back feet step directly into the tracks of its front feet, making it look like it only leaves a single line of tracks.

This animal's front paws look like a person's hand, with five fingers.

It sometimes even dunks its food in water!

Whose track is that?

→

HINT: This animal has black rings around its tail.

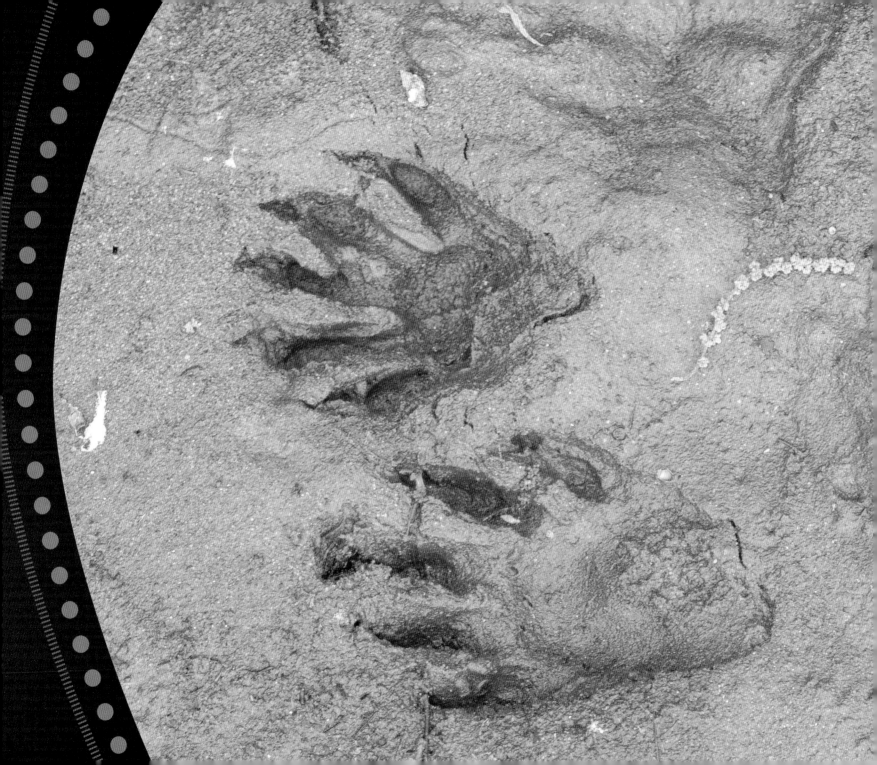

It's a
RACCOON!

The **Northern Raccoon** is also called the Common Raccoon. It has a cute black mask around its eyes that makes it look like a bank robber in a cartoon. Raccoons often live near people because we throw a lot of food into the garbage, where raccoons find it.

This animal's feet are good for walking and even better for swimming.

Its toes are connected by webbing.

Whose track is that?

HINT: This animal has feathers and honks!

It's a CANADA GOOSE!

The **Canada Goose** lives in large families; the male and female lead the babies around, so you might find a lot of tracks. When it walks on land, it waddles because its big feet get in the way.

This animal has large, round feet with long, sharp claws.

Its tracks are bigger than your hand.

Whose track is that?

HINT: This animal loves to eat honey, berries, and bugs!

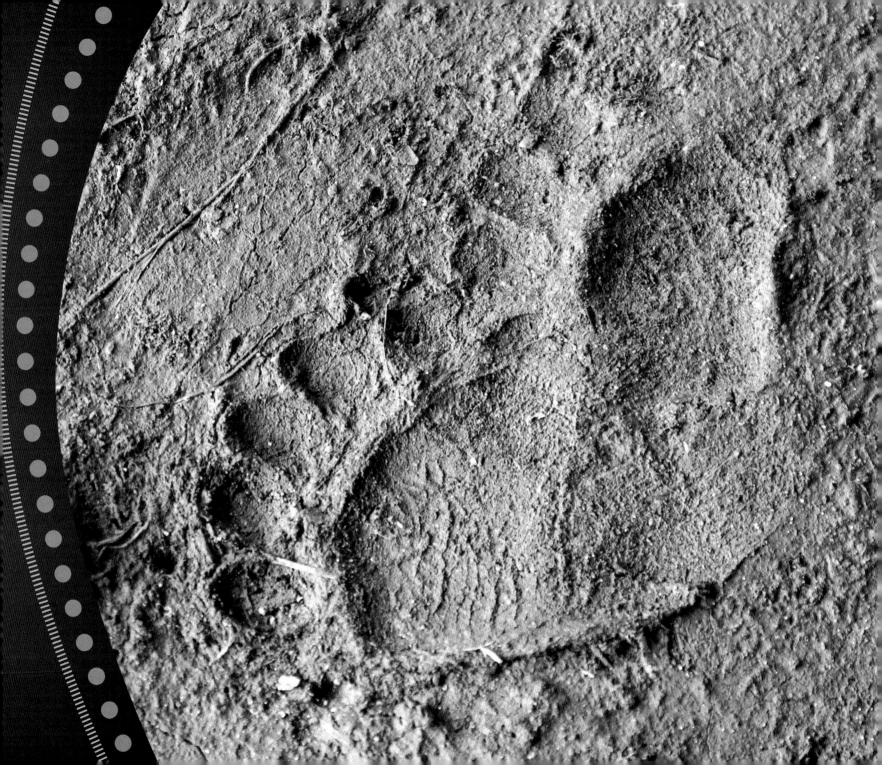

It's a BEAR!

The **American Black Bear** is the most common bear in America. Bears have long, sharp claws, and you can see claw marks in its tracks. Large male bears also often mark trees by using their teeth or claws. This helps it communicate with other bears and shows other bears how big and strong it is.

These tracks are small and oval, and they often show this animal's nails.

You might see these tracks in your yard, at a park, or at the beach.

Whose track is that?

→

HINT: This animal might live in your house!

It's a DOG!

Dogs are closely related to the Gray Wolf, and they started living with people at least 20,000 years ago. There are many different kinds of dogs. Finding dog prints is easy at parks and in backyards; if it's muddy outside, your dog might even make tracks inside!

This animal's front paw track is tiny compared to its huge back foot.

Its large, flat tail leaves a track too.

Whose track is that?

HINT: This animal has large front teeth.

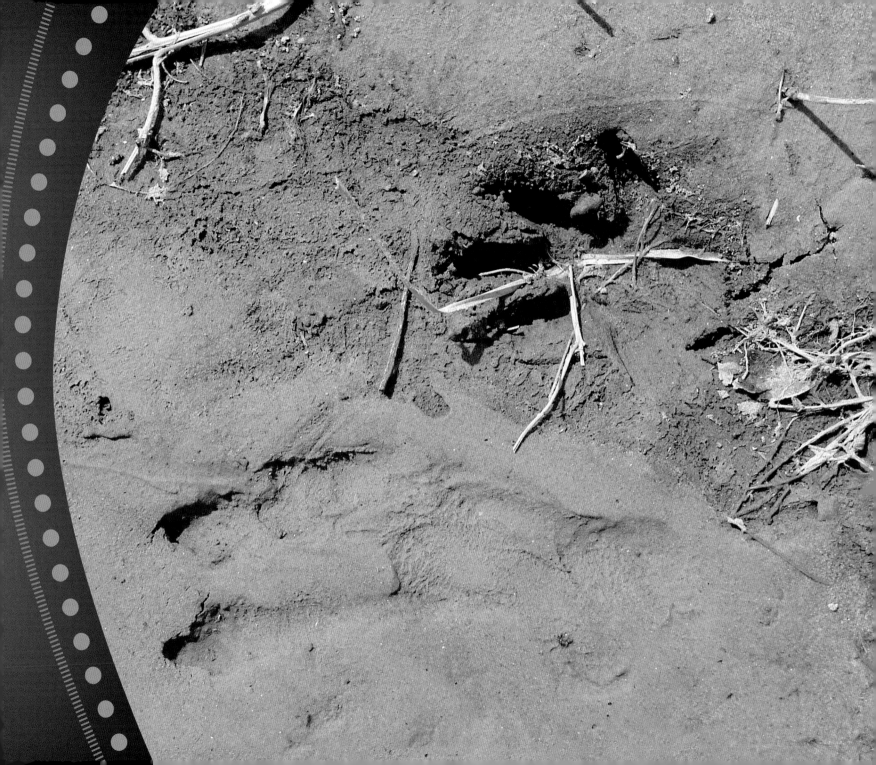

It's a
BEAVER!

The **North American Beaver** constructs special structures called dams, creating a small pond where its family can live. It spends a lot of time in the water, so look for tracks near streams and rivers.

You can see this animal's tracks when it migrates back home.

Its tracks are tiny and thin, which can make them hard to see.

Whose track is that?

HINT: This animal often runs for short distances before stopping to look for worms.

It's a
ROBIN!

When an **American Robin** runs across your lawn and turns its head, it's not listening for worms. Instead, it's looking for them, as its eyes are located on the side of its head.

When this animal runs, it's more like hopping, with its feet side by side.

Sometimes, just for fun, it slides on its belly instead of running.

Whose track is that?

HINT: This furry animal likes to have fun and play.

It's an OTTER!

In winter, **River Otters** often like to have fun by sliding down snowy hills on their bellies, just like kids going sledding. Otters don't stay in one place for very long, instead running and jumping along the edges of streams and lakes. Its tracks are always near water, so look in mud or snow along rivers and streams.

This animal's back feet are huge, helping it jump very far.

If it sits on a lily pad, you can't see its tracks at all.

Whose track is that?

→

HINT: When it leaps, sometimes it splashes into the water.

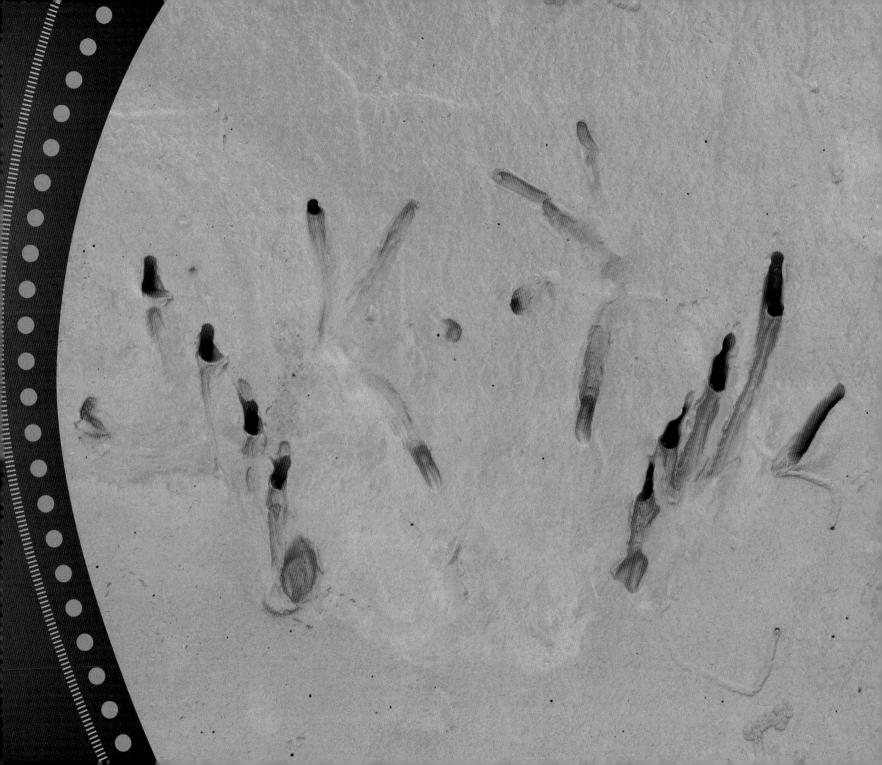

It's a BULLFROG!

The **American Bullfrog** is the largest frog in North America. It can be bigger than a dinner plate. A bullfrog's front toes are not webbed, but the back toes are.

How Big Is
YOUR TRACK?

EARTHWORM

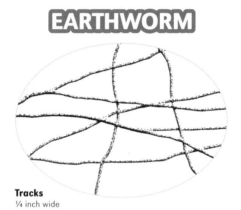

Tracks
¼ inch wide

DEER

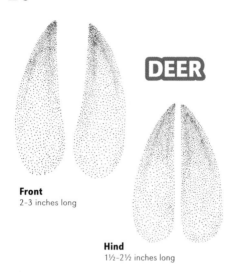

Front
2–3 inches long

Hind
1½–2½ inches long

BOBCAT

Front
1½–2 inches long

Hind
1½–2½ inches long

RACCOON

Front
2½–3 inches long

Hind
3½–4½ inches long

CANADA GOOSE

Tracks
3½–4½ inches long

BEAR

Front
4 inches long

Hind
7–9 inches long

0 inches 1 2 3 4 5 6 7 8 9

DOG

Front
2–3 inches long

Hind
2–3 inches long

BEAVER

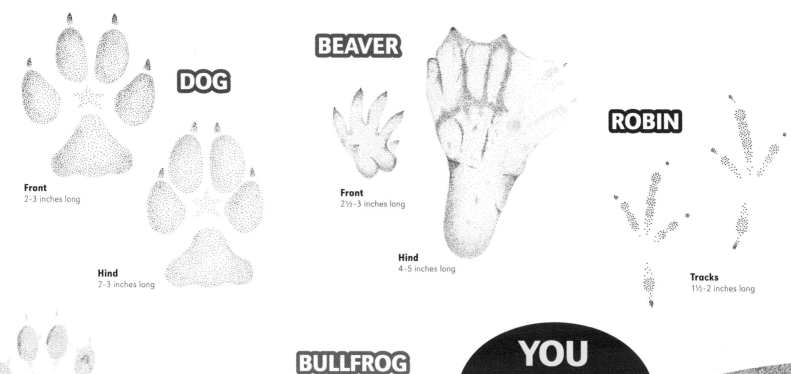

Front
2½–3 inches long

Hind
4–5 inches long

ROBIN

Tracks
1½–2 inches long

OTTER

Front
2½–3 inches long

Hind
3–3½ inches long

BULLFROG

Front
1½–2¼ inches long

Hind
2½–4 inches long

YOU

Measure your hand or your foot using this ruler. How big would your track be?

0 1 2 3 4 5

About the Author

Naturalist, wildlife photographer and writer Stan Tekiela is the author of the popular Wildlife Appreciation book series that includes *Bird Migration*. Stan has authored more than 190 educational books, including field guides, quick guides, nature books, children's books, playing cards and more, presenting many species of animals and plants.

With a Bachelor of Science degree in Natural History from the University of Minnesota and as an active professional naturalist for more than 30 years, Stan studies and photographs wildlife throughout the United States and Canada. He has received various national and regional awards for his books and photographs. Also a well-known columnist and radio personality, his syndicated column appears in more than 25 newspapers, and his wildlife programs are broadcast on a number of Midwest radio stations. Stan can be followed on Facebook and Twitter. He can be contacted via www.naturesmart.com.

More Children's Books from Stan

Stan Tekiela's books for children feature gorgeous photographs of real animals paired with captivating text. They introduce children to common, interesting and important types of North American animals.